Mountains
Mists and
Mystery

Four seasons of the mountain, four seasons of the heart

Mountains Mists and Mystery

Compiled and photographed by JACINTA SHAILER SGS

SPECTRUM PUBLICATIONS, MELBOURNE

First published 1995
by Spectrum Publications Pty Ltd
PO Box 75, Richmond Victoria Australia 3121
Ph: (03) 429 1404; Fax: (03) 428 9407

Production by Island Graphics Pty Ltd
Printed in Hong Kong

Book design: Peter Shaw
Typesetting: Scott Howard
Photographs: Jacinta Shailer
Author Photograph: Yamato Nagashima

ISBN 0 86786 103 7

CONTENTS

To my dear friends
both in Japan and in Australia
who opened my eyes to the
wonder of Nature

ACKNOWLEDGEMENTS

It is difficult to express one's gratitude to all the people who, either by their special help, comments or encouragement, have contributed to the writing of this book. I am grateful to those publishers, Charles E. Tuttle Publishing Co., Inc. Tokyo, Kodansha International Ltd. Tokyo, and Bear & Co., Santa Fe, USA, who readily gave me permission to use the quotes used in this book. I would like to thank Kazuko Yamamoto, in particular, Julian McKenna SGS and Hiro Kageyama SGS too, for the translation into Japanese of the European Mystics. To Benedicta Hui SGS, Maria Theresia Hiranabe SGS and Kumi Sakamoto, I am grateful for their calligraphy and preparing the Japanese texts. The staff of Niagara Photographics, Danielle, Steve, and Dave, who were ever ready to oblige with speed and expertise on every occasion, deserve many thanks. William Giles of Production Art Services quietly tutored me in writing my first 'mock-up' and deserves thanks for that. I also wish to thank George Zdenkowski for his legal advice, and Dianne Johnson for her invaluable help with naming the wildflowers of the Blue Mountains, as well as her ideas in other areas. Carmel Glover, by her expertise in beautifully typing the original English texts, gave a new vision of layout and has my warmest thanks. Maria Rohr, of Spectrum publications, gave me new hope when she told me over the phone she was 'savouring' my manuscript which had just come into her hands. Sean McDonagh, my first teacher to alert me to the ecological crisis threatening our earth, has very kindly written the Foreword. I am grateful that he could find time in his busy schedule to do this for me. To the one who discovered my gift for photography, Yamato Nagashima, who suggested I write this book, gave me a sense of direction with regard to colour and theme, while at the same time supporting my every effort, I wish to express my deep gratitude. To my own Sisters of the Good Samaritan who sent me on mission to Japan where I was initiated into the beauty of Nature, and who have not only encouraged me during the long period of preparation of the book, but who have also so generously jointly published this work together with Spectrum publishers I wish to express my loving gratitude.

FOREWORD

In 1992 the Union of Concerned Scientists, a worldwide association of scientists, including 99 Nobel Prize winners, warned that the Earth's peoples have no more than one or two decades left to avoid global ecological collapse.

The scientists pointed out that humans and the natural world are on a collision course. Human activity, especially in so-called 'developed' countries, is inflicting harsh and often irreversible damage on the air we breathe, the waters that quench our thirst, the soils that sustain us, and on our fellow creatures, through the massive rise in the rate of extinction. They pointed out that the Earth's ability to provide for the increased needs of humans and to absorb our pollution is finite.

The scientists concluded that a great change in our stewardship of the earth and the life on it is needed if vast human misery is to be avoided and our global home on this planet is not be irretrievably mutilated.

In recent years many people have become more aware of the destruction of the rainforest, the depletion of the ozone layer, global warming and the poisoning of our seas and lands. Often people are frightened by this knowledge and clamour for change.

We all know that fear can motivate a certain amount of change in human behaviour. But as sensitive religious leaders from Jesus to the Buddha remind us, fear is not an adequate wellspring from which to sustain permanent change or conversion. This must spring from love.

This is why Jacinta Shailer's book *Mountains, Mists and Mystery* is so valuable. She is in love with the infinite variety of the natural world. Her exquisite photos capture the beauty of Nature in the autumn leaves, the sparkle of dewdrops on the leaves, the delicate butterfly, the beautiful flowers and the majesty of the mountains. She marries this visible beauty with insightful texts, expertly chosen from both Japanese and European poets and mystics.

As I read the poems and studied the photos I felt touched and drawn by the magic of nature and its irresistible allurement. I am convinced that this re-enchantment with Nature, be it in the flight of a gannet or the beauty of a flower, is a prerequisite for enabling modern human beings to break out of our autistic and destructive relationship with the rest of creation. It is only by removing the scales from our eyes that we can really appreciate the present devastation, begin to heal the damage and live in harmony with the rest of creation.

For this reason we are all very much indebted to Jacinta. Like a true artist her sensitive presentation and engaging narrative can help others reconnect with nature. It is obvious, both from the texts and the photos, that her journey of enlightenment was very much facilitated and enriched by her experience of Japanese culture. One can only hope that Japanese readers will also be encouraged by the book to challenge the activities of Japanese Transnational Corporations who are very much to the fore in the destruction of the rainforest in southeast Asia, Latin America and Papua New Guinea.

Sean McDonagh SSC
Ireland
May 12, 1994

PREFACE

This book is about Nature. In particular, it is about Nature in the Blue Mountains of Australia which is the theme of the book's photography. The poems that accompany the photography, are about Nature too, but from two different cultures, one European, and the other Japanese. These poems were written in the period of the tenth century to the seventeenth. By the choice of photograph accompanying the word in the two languages, Japanese and English, I am hoping to open up new vistas of understanding between Japan and the English speaking world.

I owe my own love of Nature to the Japanese people with whom I lived for twenty years. Any attunement I have with the seasons, any sensitivity to the first blossoms of spring, I am indebted to the gentle and pervasive influence of my Japanese friends. By their daily attention to the subtle movements of Nature, they initiated me into a world to which I had been closed and unaware. These friends of mine have led me to appreciate, not only the beauty of our delicate, beautiful wildflowers and our breath-taking landscapes, but they have also helped me understand something of the intimate relationship bonding us as companions of the one creation.

The Japanese poems I have chosen are from the tenth to the seventeenth century. Though not all the Japanese poems are HAIKU, the majority is in this form. It is amazing that within this compact structure of three lines of five-seven-five syllables, such a variety of thoughts and feelings can be expressed. Matsuo Basho (1644–1694), the master of HAIKU, was so intimately attuned to his experience, often very mundane and commonplace in itself, that it explodes within him and us, opening up a new world.

Nature and the seasons are integral to the HAIKU. So it is not surprising then, that the composition of the book follows the pattern of the four seasons. This does not mean that in the section depicting winter, for example, there are only winter flowers and scenes of the Blue Mountains in winter, though it may be the case. What I have tried to do, is unite the poems of both East and West with photography that gives a flavour of the season. The title of each seasonal segment also gives some indication of the thrust in mind. The Japanese title of this book is 'The Four Seasons of the Mountain, the Four Seasons of the Heart'. This indicates that it can be read for its own pictorial enjoyment, but there is the challenge to savour the book with the heart, and with an intuitive inner sense.

The European poets of the Middle Ages that I have chosen, Hildegard of Bingen (1098–1179), Mechtild of Magdeburg (1210–1297), Meister Eckhart (1260–1325), and Julian of Norwich (1340–1419), are noted for their environmental wisdom. Nature played a vital and meaningful role in living their daily lives and in bringing them to a deeper encounter with a personal God. For the Japanese poets, especially Basho, it was in and through Nature, that they hoped to obtain SATORI, or enlightenment. Now and then one feels Basho intuitively caught a glimpse of the goal of his yearning as is exemplified in this poem he wrote while visiting the Kasuragi Mountains.

> *All the more I wish to see*
> *Among those blossoms at dawn*
> *The face of the god.*

The belief of the people of the time was that the god of the word who resided there, would only inspire at night because his face was so ugly he had no wish to be seen. But Basho is so entranced with the beauty of the surrounding mountains, that he thinks the god should be beautiful too, and be happy to reveal his face at the dawning of the day.

Taking a very broad view of the place of Nature in the writings of the European and Japanese poets mentioned in this book, I find it very interesting to compare the two. In the Europeans I pick up a real experience of hope and joy in the beauties of creation, coupled with compassion for the earth. I feel, with regard to the Japanese writings, that several are brushed with a melancholic touch. In many of them there is an explicit portrayal of loneliness. However, I sense that in creation, be it the chirping cicada, or the crow resting on a dead branch, the Japanese find solace and peace. But, what they all have in common, be they European or Japanese, is an experience of companionship with the universe. The wonder and beauty of the world has impregnated their beings and flowed into their poetry and life. This is their gift to us.

My hope is that by reading a few excerpts from the writings of these great people of different cultural and religious backgrounds, we may be reminded of the enriching, global heritage which is ours. I also hope that with the added dimension of the photography of one of the most beautiful and abundant wildflower areas in Australia, the Blue Mountains, we may appreciate an Australian heritage that, sad to say, is being diminished daily. May our own lives be more gently moulded by the love of Nature as experienced by these great men and women of the East and the West as we savour their words in the company of photography of the South.

Jacinta Shailer
Blue Mountains
May 1994

読者の皆様へ

　ブルーマウンテンは、霧と神秘につつまれています。四季折々に変わる自然と野草の写真にそれを留めてみました。また、そこに表れたメッセージを、百人一首や俳句、ヨーロッパの中世の作品から引用しました。

　私は二〇年間過ごした日本で、日本の人々から自然の美しさに初めて目を覚まされ、写真を写す喜びを教わりました。そこで日本の皆様に感謝を込めてこの本を贈りたいと思います。　文化や宗教的背景が違っても日本とヨーロッパの人々が共にもっている宇宙との一体感と、南半球オーストラリアのブルーマウンテンに残されている自然の美しさを味わっていただければ幸いです。

　　　　　　ブルーマウンテンにて
　　　　　　ジャシンタ・シェイラー

天地の恵みを味わうとき

Savouring the gifts of the Cosmos

Autumn Leaves, The Avenue, Mt Wilson

Overlooking Wollangambe River, Mt Wilson

The path of which I have spoken
is beautiful
and pleasant
and joyful
and familiar

Meister Eckhart

私の語った道は
美しく
快く
喜びに満ち
通い慣れている
　　　エックハルト

Perry's Lookdown, Blackheath

白露に
風の吹きしく
秋の野は
つらぬきとめぬ
玉ぞちりける
文屋朝康

Grevillea biternata

*T*his lovely morn the dewdrops flash
Like diamonds on the grass —
A blaze of sparkling jewels? But
The autumn wind, alas!
Scatters them as I pass.

Asayasu Bunya, Ninth Century

Hakea leaf

I govern the light of the skies,
I govern the trees, grasses,
And all other earthly greenings.

Hildegard of Bingen

私は
大空の光をつかさどり
木や草をつかさどり
すべての地上の緑を
支配します
ヒルデガルト

Persoonia levis, Geebung Broad Leaf

*All creation is gifted with the
ecstasy of God's light.*

Hildegard of Bingen

万物は
神の光の悦びに
あずかっています
　　　ヒルデガルト

Banksia serrata, Old Man Banksia

Banksia serrata, Old Man Banksia

Fungus, Megalong Valley

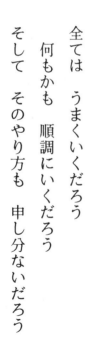

*All will be well
and all will be well
and every manner of things
will be well.*

Julian of Norwich

全ては　うまくいくだろう
何もかも　順調にいくだろう
そして　そのやり方も　申し分ないだろう
ジューリアン

24

Cahill's Lookout, Megalong Valley

おお、満月となった月よ！
おお、輝く荘厳な太陽よ！
　　　　メヒトヒルト

O full moon in your course!
O glorious sun in your shining!

Mechtild of Magdeburg

*T*wo decorated lanterns
Competing to reveal the depth
of love.
Dewdrops and bush clover
Wrestling with each other
In a perfect match.

Matsuo Basho

燈籠ふたつに情けくらぶる　杜國

つゆ萩のすまふ力を撰ばれず　芭蕉

Banksia ericafolia, Heath Banksia

On the Stone Mountain
It is whiter than the stones:
Autumnal wind.

Matsuo Basho

石山の
いしより白し
秋のかぜ
芭蕉

Dogface Rock, Narrow Neck

Leaf Pool, Kanangra Boyd National Park

All red with leaves Tatsuta's stream
So softly purls along.
The everlasting Gods themselves,
Who judge 'twixt right and wrong,
Ne'er heard so sweet a song.

Nari-Hira Ariwara, 825–880 A.D.

千早ぶる
神代よも聞かず
龍田川
からくれないに
水くくるとは
　　在原業平

Drenched passersby:
They are so beautiful —
Bush clover in the rain.

Matsuo Basho

ぬれて行

人もおかしや

雨の萩

芭蕉

Eucalyptus tips

Jamison Valley, Wentworth Falls

arth cannot escape heaven
Flee it by going up,
or flee it by going down,
heaven still invades the earth,
energizes it,
makes it sacred.

Meister Eckhart

Jamison Valley — Evening Storm

地は天を避けることはできない
上に上って逃げようとも
下に潜って逃げようとも

天はそれでも
地に入り込み
精気を与え
聖なるものに　する

　　　エックハルト

Cliff Walk, Wentworth Falls

巡礼者は　山頂をめざして
必死に登ります
そして　断崖から落ちないように
注意して降ります
魂も　また　そのようにするのです
メヒトヒルト

The soul does as pilgrims do
who have eagerly climbed to the summit
of a mountain
they descend with care
lest they fall over a precipice.

Mechtild of Magdeburg

Hanging Rock, Blackheath

Red Lacewing

The fragrant orchid
Into a butterfly's wings
It breathes the incense.

Matsuo Basho

蘭の香や
蝶のつばさに
たき物のす
　　芭蕉

*T*his autumn
Why am I ageing so?
Flying towards the clouds, a bird.

Matsuo Basho

此の秋は
何で年よる
雲に鳥
芭蕉

Valley of the Waters, Wentworth Falls

35

Evening — Govett's Leap

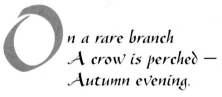n a rare branch
A crow is perched —
Autumn evening.

Matsuo Basho

枯れ朶に
鳥のとまりけり
秋の暮

　　芭蕉

Jamison Valley, Wentworth Falls

*T*he rain, which fell from passing showers,
Like drops of dew, still lies
Upon the fir-tree needles, and
The mists of evening rise
Up to the autumn skies.

The Priest Jaku-ren, Twelfth Century

Govett's Leap, Blackheath

むらさめの
つゆもまだひぬ
槙の葉に
霧立ちのぼる
秋の夕暮れ
　　　寂蓮法師

Echo Point, Katoomba

闇の中で新しい命への戦いが
されているとき

Struggling for new life in the darkness

Cliff Drive, Leura

Echo Point, Katoomba

Olearia quercifolia, Oak-leaved Daisy-bush

私たちは
神の恩寵のすべてを
心に刻みこまなければなりません
メヒトヒルト

We ought to imprint
all God's gifts
into our hearts.

Mechtild of Magdeburg

Olearia quercifolia, Oak-leaved Daisy-bush

Ruined Castle, Katoomba

A cloud, trying to enwrap
The moonbeams, momentarily fails —
A winter shower.

Tsubio Tokoku (1658–1690)

つ、みかねて
月とり落とす
霽かな
しぐれ

杜國

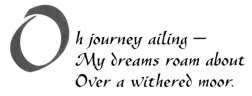

Oh journey ailing —
My dreams roam about
Over a withered moor.

Matsuo Basho

旅に病んで
夢は枯れ野を
かけ廻る
芭蕉

Banksia spinulosa, Hairpin Banksia

Oh stormy winds, bring up the clouds,
And paint the heavens grey:
Lest these fair maids of form divine
Should angel wings display
And fly far far away.

Munesade Yoshimune (Bishop Henjo), died 865

天つ風
雲の通い路
吹きとじよ
乙女の姿
しばしとどめむ
僧正遍昭

Escarpment, Wentworth Falls

Belltrees, Bell's Line of Road

木枯に
岩吹きとがる
杉間かな

　　芭蕉

Against the wintry gust
How sharp are the rocks
Amid the cedars!

Matsuo Basho

This firmament is an all-encompassing circle
No one can say where this wheel begins or ends.

Hildegard of Bingen

この天空は
ひたすら廻る円い輪

この車輪は
どこから始まり
どこで終わるのか

だれにも言えません
ヒルデガルト

Jamison Valley, Wentworth Falls

*The fullness of joy
is
to behold
God
in everything*

Julian of Norwich

Actinotus forsythii, Pink Flannel Flower

完全な喜びは
すべての中に
神を　見ることです

ジューリアン

*T*he earth should not be injured.
The earth should not be destroyed.

Hildegard of Bingen

Ingar Picnic Area, Blue Mountains National Park

地球は
破壊されてはならないのです
ヒルデガルト

地球は
傷つけられてはなりません

The blossom's tint is washed away
By heavy showers of rain:
My charms, which once I prized
so much,
Are also on the wane —
Both bloomed, alas! in vain.

Komachi Ono, 834–880

花の色は
うつりにけりな
いたづらに
わが身世にふる
ながめせしまに

小野小町

Petrophile pulchella, Conesticks

Weeping Rock, Wentworth Falls

Leptospermum lanigerum var. macrocarpum, Tea Tree

Leptospermum lanigerum var. macrocarpum, Tea Tree

私にわかることは
私の生きる道は　ただ一つ
バラのように
なぜだろうといぶかることなく
生きていくことだ
　　　　エックハルト

*T*his I know.
that the only way to live
is like the rose
which lives without a why.

Meister Eckhart

Actinotus helianthi, Flannel Flower

*H*ow should one live?
*L*ive welcoming to all.

Mechtild of Magdeburg

どのようにして
生きていけばよいのでしょうか？

すべてを　喜んで受け入れ
生きていくのです

メヒトヒルト

Actinotus helianthi, Flannel Flower

*The sea darkens
And a wild duck's call
Is faintly white.*

Matsuo Basho

海くれて
鴨のこゑ
ほのかに白し
芭蕉

Blue Mountains National Park

Wentworth Falls Lake

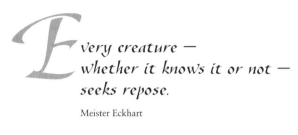

*E*very creature —
whether it knows it or not —
seeks repose.

Meister Eckhart

Vindula arsinoe, Cruiser

Caterpillar, Henson's Glen

あらゆる被造物は
それを意識しようと　しまいと
平安を求めている

エックハルト

*G*aze at the sun.
See the moon and the stars.
Gaze at the beauty of earth's
greenings.

Hildegard of Bingen

Echo Point, Katoomba

見詰めてごらん　太陽を
見てごらん　月や星々を
見詰めてごらん
地球が青々とよみがえる美しさを
　　　　　　　　ヒルデガルト

Billardiera scandens, Apple Berry

Spring

生まれいずる希望に踊るとき

Dancing in paths of creative hope

Styphelia tubiflora, Red Five-corners

Detronica phoenica, Flame Robin

The spring has come, and once again
The sun shines in the sky:
So gently smile the heavens, that
It almost makes me cry.
When blossoms droop and die.

Tomonori Kino, Ninth Century

久かたの
光のどけき
春の日に
しづ心なく
花の散るらむ

紀　友則

Bauera rubioides, Dog Rose

Bauera rubioides, Dog Rose

Kunzea capitata, Pink Kunzea

Come. Love!
Sing on
let me hear you sing this song
Sing for joy
and laugh
for I the Creator
am truly subject to all creatures.

Mechtild of Magdeburg

Mirbelia rubiifolia and *Dampiera stricta*

愛する者よ　おいで
お前の歌を　聞かせておくれ
喜びの歌を

笑っておくれ

私、造り主は
すべて生あるものに
心から尽くすのですから
　　　メヒトヒルト

Dendrobium kingianum, Pink Rock Orchid

From which tree's bloom
It comes, I do not know:
This fragrance!

Matsuo Basho

何の木の
花とはしらず
匂かな

芭蕉

山路来きて
何やらゆかし
すみれ草

芭蕉

A long the mountain road
Somehow it tugs my heart:
A wild violet.

Matsuo Basho

Tetratheca ericafolia, Black-eyed Susan

All the more I wish to see
Among those blossoms at dawn
The face of god.

Matsuo Basho

Boronia microphylla, Small-leafed Boronia

Boronia microphylla, Small-leafed Boronia

神の顔
花に明行
なほ見たし
　芭蕉

The day of my spiritual awakening
was the day I saw
and knew I saw
all things in God
and God in all things.

Mechtild of Magdeburg

Eriostemon myropoides, Native Daphne

Eriostemon myropoides, Native Daphne

私の霊的な目覚めの日は
神のうちに　万物を見
万物の中に　神を見た日であり
そのことを知った日です
　　　　　メヒトヒルト

After the chimes fade
Cherry fragrance continues:
Evening dusk.

Matsuo Basho

鐘消て
花の香は撞
夕べかな
芭蕉

Valley of the Waters, Wentworth Falls

Valley of the Waters, Wentworth Falls

創造されたものの美しさに
感嘆するとき

そして　造り主の美しい摂理を
賛美するとき

これが救いである

　　　　エックハルト

Thelymitra ixiodes, Spotted Sun Orchid Buds

Wahlenbergia stricta, Tall Bluebell

This is salvation:
when we marvel at the beauty
of created things
and praise the beautiful providence
of their Creator.

Meister Eckhart

Thelymitra ixiodes, Spotted Sun Orchid

Six tan of farmland
Covered with violets and red clover
Joyously
The skylark sings:
Chiri chiri...

Matsuo Basho

Thelymitra ixiodes, Spotted Sun Orchid

五形菫の畠六反
うれしげに囀る雲雀ちりちりと　　とこく

芭蕉

85

Stypandra caespitosa, Tufted Blue Lily

F idelity sees God
and Wisdom keeps God close by
and from these two comes Love —
a delight in God
completely steeped in wonder.

Julian of Norwich

Thysanotus tuberosus, Fringed Violet

誠実は　神を見

英知は　神を近づけます

そして　このふたつから
愛が生じます

愛とは
神のなかの喜び
完全な神秘の浸り

ジューリアン

Patersonia sericea, Native Iris

Thysanotus tuberosus, Fringed Violet

W*e must trust and be glad for everything.*

Julian of Norwich

私たちは　全てを信じ

全てを　喜ばなければなりません

ジューリアン

Stypandra caespitosa, Tufted Blue Lily

Patersonia sericea, Native Iris

Dianella revoluta berries, Black-anther Flax Lily

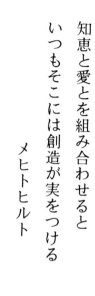

賢者が
知恵と愛とを組み合わせると
いつもそこには創造が実をつける
メヒトヒルト

*W*henever genius
combines wisdom
and love,
There
Creation bears fruit.

Mechtild of Magdeburg

Dianella revoluta berries, Black-anther Flax Lily

夏

Summer

畏敬と叡知の中で成熟するとき

Maturing in awe and compassionate wisdom

Platycircus elegans, Crimson Rosella

Callistemon citrinus, Crimson Bottlebrush

Horseshoe Falls, Blackheath

The blowing wind,
the mild, moist air,
the exquisite greening
of trees and grasses —

Hildegard of Bingen

吹く風よ
穏やかで　潤いをおびた大気よ
草木の鮮やかな緑よ
　　　　　ヒルデガルト

Xanthorrhoea media, Grass Tree

天は草にみずみずしい露を与え
地のすべては
神の恵に歓喜します

ヒルデガルト

*T*he heavens gift the grass
with moist dew.
The entire earth rejoices.

Hildegard of Bingen

Ingar Picnic Area, Blue Mountains National

*T*he air is life,
greening and blossoming.
The waters flow with life.
The sun is lit with life.

Hildegard of Bingen

大気は　いのち
草木を緑に萌えさせ　花を咲かせる
いのちにより　水は流れ
いのちにより　太陽は輝く
ヒルデガルト

Wentworth Falls

蝶の飛ぶ
ばかり野中の
日かげかな
　芭蕉

Cairns Birdwing

A butterfly flits
All alone — and on the field,
A shadow in the sunlight.

Matsuo Basho

Red Lacewing

Drosera spathulata, Sundew

私は　雨
草を生きる喜びに
笑いの声をあげさせる
露から落ちる　雨

ヒルデガルト

I
am the rain
coming down from the dew
that causes the grasses to
with the joy of life.

Hildegard of Bingen

Banksia marginata, Silver Banksia

O
lovely rose on the thorn!
O hovering bee in the honey!
O pure dove in your being!
O glorious sun in your setting!
O full moon in your course!
From you
I your God will never turn away.

Mechtild of Magdeburg

とげの上の美しいバラ！
蜜にむらがるハチ！
清いハト！
沈み行く荘厳な太陽！
満月になった月！
おまえ達の神である私は
決しておまえ達から顔を背けることはないであろう
メヒトヒルト

Grevillea acanthifolia ssp. acanthifolia

Sunset, Megalong Valley

いのちは　今　弱々しく見えます
もはや
神の火のような愛に
耐えさせるだけの若さがないほどに
メヒトヒルト

*L*ife appears powerless
now that it no longer has youth.
to help it endure
the fiery love of God

Mechtild of Magdeburg

Beauty in Maturity

*I have often said
that God is creating the entire
universe
fully and totally
in this present now.*

Meister Eckhart

私は　たびたび言った
神はいま　この時
全宇宙を
満ち足りた　完全なものに
お造りになっている　と
　　　　エックハルト

Earth Star

I am the breeze
that nurtures all things green
I encourage blossoms to flourish
with ripening fruits.

Hildegard of Bingen

わたしは　風
すべての緑を育み
花を咲かせ
実を熟させます
ヒルデガルト

Drosera binata, Sundew

Billardiera scandens, Apple Berry

Callociphalon fimbriatum, male Gang-gang Cockatoo

How does God come to us?
Like dew on the flowers
Like the song of the birds!

Mechtild of Magdeburg

Lambertia formosa, Honey Flower

神は　どのようにして
私たちのところに　来るのだろう？
花に宿る露のように
小鳥のさえずる歌のように！
メヒトヒルト

Lambertia formosa, Honey Flower

私は見た
善きもの
精気あふるるものは
総て
神である

　　ジューリアン

Lambertia formosa, Honey Flower

I saw that God is everything
that is good and energizing.

Julian of Norwich

Dragonfly

Every single creature is full of God and is a book about God.

Meister Eckhart

生あるもの　ひとつひとつが
神に満ちあふれている
そして　そのひとつひとつは
神についての本である
　　　　　　　エックハルト

Telopea speciosissima, Waratah

*T*here is no creation
that does not have a radiance,
be it greenness of seed,
Blossom or beauty
It could not be creation without it.

Hildegard of Bingen

燦然とした輝きのない
被造物なんてありえない

種子の緑であれ、
華であれ、美であれ、

この輝きなくして
被造物でありえない

ヒルデガルト

Grevillea laurifolia

Telopea speciosissima, Waratah

神は言われる
　死を恐れてはなりません
　その時が来れば
　私が息を吸い込み
　あなたの魂が
　磁石にひかれる針のように
　私の許に帰ってくるからです
　　　　　メヒトヒルト

Crytostylis subulata, Cow Orchid

Crytostylis subulata, Cow Orchid

God says:
Do not fear your death.
For when that moment arrives
I will draw my breath
and your soul will come to Me
like a needle to a magnet.

Mechtild of Magdeburg

NOTES

Page ref.

18. Fox, Matthew, *Meditations with Meister Eckhart.* Santa Fe, New Mexico: Bear & Company 1983, p. 131.
19. Porter, William N., *A Hundred Verses from Old Japan.* being a translation of the *Hyaku -Nin-Isshu,* Tokyo: Charles Tuttle Company, 1979, p. 37.
20. Uhlein, Gabriele, *Meditations of Hildegard of Bingen.* Santa Fe, New Mexico: Bear & Company 1983, p. 33.
22. Uhlein, *op. cit.* p. 32.
24. Doyle, Brendan, *Meditations with Julian of Norwich,* Santa Fe, New Mexico: Bear & Company 1983, p. 48.
25. Woodruff, Sue, *Meditations with Mechtild of Magdeburg.* Santa Fe, New Mexico; Bear & Company 1982, p. 51.
26. Ueda, Makoto, *The Master Haiku Poet Matsuo Basho.* Tokyo: Kodansha International Ltd. 1970, p. 75.
27. Ueda, *op. cit.* p. 54.
28. Porter, *op. cit.* p. 17.
29. Ueda, *op. cit.* p. 58.
30. Fox, *op. cit.* p. 15.
32. Woodruff, *op. cit.* p. 59.
34. Ueda, *op. cit.* p. 48.
35. Ueda, *op. cit.* p. 34.
36. Ueda, *op. cit.* p. 44.
38. Porter, *op. cit.* p. 87.
44. Woodruff, *op. cit.* p. 44.
46. Ueda, *op. cit.* p. 71.
47. Ueda, *op. cit.* p. 35.
48. Porter, *op. cit.* p. 12.
49. Ueda, *op. cit.* p. 54.
50. Uhlein, *op. cit.* p. 29.
51. Doyle, *op. cit.* p. 60.

52. Uhlein, *op. cit.* p. 78.
54. Porter. *op. cit.* p. 9.
57. Fox, *op. cit.* p.30.
58. Woodruff, *op. cit.* 126.
60. Ueda, *op. cit.* p. 48.
62. Fox, *op. cit.* p. 86.
64. Uhlein, *op. cit.* p. 45.
70. Porter, *op. cit.* p. 33.
72. Woodruff, *op. cit.* p. 55.
74. Ueda, *op. cit.* p. 133.
75. Ueda, *op. cit.* p. 49.
76. Ueda, *op. cit.* p. 134.
78. Woodruff, *op. cit.* p. 42.
80. Ueda, *op. cit.* p. 56.
83. Fox, *op. cit.* p. 107.
84. Ueda, *op. cit.* p. 79.
86. Doyle, *op. cit.* p. 48.
88. Doyle, *op. cit.* p. 52.
90. Woodruff, *op. cit.* p. 85.
96. Uhlein, *op. cit.* p. 47.
97. Uhlein, *op. cit.* p. 116.
98. Uhlein, *op. cit.* p. 32.
100. Ueda, *op. cit.* p. 50.
102. Uhlein, *op. cit.* p. 31.
104. Woodruff, *op. cit.* p. 35.
106. Woodruff, *op. cit.* p. 74.
107. Fox, *op. cit.* p. 24.
108. Uhlein, *op. cit.* p. 31.
111. Woodruff, *op. cit.* p. 36.
113. Doyle, *op. cit.* p. 24 .
115. Fox, *op. cit.* p. 14 .
116. Uhlein, *op. cit.* p. 24.
119. Woodruff, *op. cit.* p. 80.

10870

242
Sha

Date Due		
D. Keenan		
B Hansson		
'6 MAR 1958		
Debi	CANCELLED	